LISTENING TO
THE VOICE OF GOD

SHIRLEY SMLTH

WESTBOW
PRESS
A DIVISION OF THOMAS NELSON

WestBow Press books may be ordered through booksellers or by contacting:

WestBow Press
A Division of Thomas Nelson
1663 Liberty Drive
Bloomington, IN 47403
www.westbowpress.com
1-(866) 928-1240

All Scripture quotations are taken from the King James Study Bible, King James Version, Thomas Nelson, Inc., Publisher

ISBN: 978-1-4497-7427-1 (e)
ISBN: 978-1-4497-7426-4 (sc)

Library of Congress Control Number: 2012921052

Printed in the United States of America

WestBow Press rev. date:11/09/2012

To my niece, Kimberly Shepherd

Out of heaven he made thee to hear his voice,
that he might instruct thee.

—Deuteronomy 4:36

CONTENTS

PREFACE

OD DREW ME TO HIMSELF as he drew me to his Word. *Listening to the Voice of God* is an account of the living Word of God as it has enriched my life. In the fourteenth chapter of the book of Matthew, Jesus distributed fish and bread to the disciples, directing them in turn to distribute to the multitude. The pattern continues as he gives us spiritual food and calls upon us to share it with others.

In that spirit, I am sharing what he has given to me. Come along and rejoice in God's love and care. If you have not yet personally experienced new life in Jesus, may these pages help you find a new appreciation for God's Word and to seek him and his will for your life.

Thanks to Elder W. F. Faust, Jr., who has conveyed his love of and devotion to the Word of God to everyone who has sat in the congregation of the Victory in Christ Bible Church, and who has brought so much of the Scriptures to light for me.

All Scripture quotations are taken from the Holy Bible, King James Version.

INTRODUCTION

LISTENING TO THE VOICE OF God is a personal witness of God moving in my life. It is a witness of his willingness to love and care for each person born into the world. It is based on God's Word as recorded in the Holy Bible, and portrays God's gracious response to those who have faith in Jesus Christ, the Son of God.

There is a wisdom and knowledge that only God can impart. Such wisdom and knowledge exists apart from information acquired through educational training. I know, because I, as well as many other believers in Christ, laypersons like myself, have received enlightened understanding of the Word of God through the Holy Spirit that dwells within us.

God uses various means to guide us and communicate his will, including his written Word, circumstances, and strong inner convictions. He desires to speak to every heart. I have never regretted listening to his voice and walking in his way, for my life has been enriched immeasurably.

TRUE TREASURE

Look unto me, and be ye saved,
all the ends of the earth: for I am
God, and there is none else.

—*Isaiah 45:22*

CHRIST LIVES NOW! GOD PLACED these celebratory words into my mind as I awoke one Sunday morning almost twenty years ago. Thanks to God, his Son, Jesus Christ, does live. Because of Jesus Christ, we have unfathomable riches. If you have received him as your Savior, you have claimed your treasure. If you have not, you're missing more than you can imagine.

With Jesus in your life, you have access to exhilarating communication with God. Not only can you talk to God, but also God will speak to you. If you have begun your walk with Jesus, perhaps you have not yet surrendered to the point of regularly hearing God speak. Perhaps you haven't begun to listen attentively. One thing is certain: we all need to hear from God.

Why do you need to hear God speak to you? Why do you need to listen? God made each of us to live the life he created humans to live—a life dependent on him, a life lived in purity and devotion to him, trusting him to supply

✝

our needs and to grant our desires according to his will. Most of us try other routes to satisfaction, happiness, and peace, not realizing that through God the Creator, we have all of this. We need only look to him.

We all need God to help with the decisions we must make during our lives. Which job or career is right for me? Is it a good time to change my job or career? Whom should I marry? Should I move to another city? You may not be ready to believe that God is interested in these concerns, but he is. He stands ready to help. However, God requires something of us before he will take control and lead us—before we can hear him speak in the situations we face. He needs a seeking heart—a heart willing to seek to know the way to the spiritual life he has provided through his Son, Jesus Christ.

Intentional listening to God is integral to a satisfying life because our response to the words God speaks to us determines whether we receive the treasure he has for us.

The Bible is the Holy Word of God. It opens the door and shows the way to true life. We can exist physically for a lifetime without biblical knowledge and without the knowledge of God. However, because such a lifestyle is contrary to the plan God has for us, it is a meaningless lifestyle that results in a life lived in vain. Humans share many of the same experiences, whether they are living with or without God. They experience the same sensations; they create family units; they suffer the same diseases or conditions; they make moral choices. But a life lived without God misses the true substance of life. It misses what true life is all about.

To enter into the life God has prepared, we must hear and believe the Word of God. God gives us the faith we need to allow his Word to take effect in our hearts. The tenth chapter of Romans tells us what we need to hear first, and why.

> For whosoever shall call upon the name of the Lord shall be saved. How then shall they call on him in whom they have not believed? and how shall they believe in him of whom they have not heard? and how shall they hear without a preacher? So then faith cometh by hearing, and hearing by the word of God. (Romans 10:13–14, 17)

Romans 3:23 teaches that "all have sinned, and come short of the glory of God." We come into the world with a universal sin nature, separated from God by the sin that originated with his first human creations, Adam and Eve. The first thing that a merciful God wants us to listen to in his Word is the remedy for sin. This issue must be settled before we enter into the life he has prepared for us.

Most adults and many children are familiar with this verse: "For God so loved the world, that he gave his only begotten Son, that whosoever believeth in him should not perish, but have everlasting life" (John 3:26). When we listen to these words, when we are intent on understanding, these words are invaluable.

The penalty for sin is eternal death. That penalty is a debt we owe. The debt must be paid. This is why we need to hear that Jesus paid the penalty of death for each of us by dying for each of us. Through his death, each of us is forgiven. In his love, God bids us to respond to that message by accepting the gift of salvation he has given us through Jesus, for the gift belongs to no one before it is accepted.

We accept God's gift when we confess (or agree with God) that we are sinners. Once we've prayed sincerely, asking to be forgiven, we are no longer under the penalty of eternal death. Even when biological death ends our physical existence on earth, our spirits will live eternally with God. Not only are we no longer subject to sin's penalty, but we are also freed from its power. This means that we are no longer enslaved under our original sin nature. We are free to live for God.

This verse expresses the majestic beauty of God's justification: "Being justified freely by his grace through the redemption that is in Christ Jesus" (Romans 3:24). In the grand picture of justification, God sees us as righteous the moment we believe.

God's favor is a gift of grace that we neither earn nor deserve. The righteousness of Jesus becomes our righteousness, although we face a lifetime of learning to live so that our lives "adorn the doctrine of God our Savior in all things" (Titus 2:10). This is life to the fullest.

Another part of God's great gift is the gift of the Holy Spirit. The Holy Spirit takes residence within our hearts when we believe. Peter's response to the crowd that had listened to the Word of God and couldn't wait to experience the Jesus they had heard about while witnessing the manifestation of the Spirit was as follows: "Repent, and be baptized every one of you in the name of Jesus Christ for the remission of sins, and ye shall receive the gift of the Holy Ghost" (Acts 2:38).

The Holy Spirit is our helper. The Holy Spirit gives us the power to live lives that are pleasing to God. The Holy

Spirit is the source of our power over sin. Jesus died and rose again, and he now sits at the right hand of God the Father. While he walked on earth, Jesus told his disciples that the Holy Spirit would be sent to be with them when he departed. Listen to a portion of the assurance he left with the men who followed him: "Nevertheless I tell you the truth; It is expedient for you that I go away: for if I go not away, the Comforter will not come unto you; but if I depart, I will send him unto you" (John 16:7).

We learn basic rules of right and wrong when we are very young. Our consciences guide us throughout life. But to know truth, to know right from wrong according to God's Word, we need the Holy Spirit of God. The Holy Spirit continually works in us, transforming us according to the will of God and empowering us to do God's will.

We no longer desire to immerse ourselves in sensual pleasures. Although temptation may flash an alluring smile, by the power of God, we do not yield. We are free to live for God, to delight ourselves in him. We are ready to hear God speak in all the affairs of life, and he delights in speaking to us. This is true treasure.

LISTENING FOR GOD'S VOICE

But my God shall supply all your
need according to his riches
in glory by Christ Jesus.

—Philippians 4:19

GOD SPEAKS TO US PRIMARILY through his written Word, the Holy Bible. God's Word gives life. Therefore, it deserves more than our taking a quick excursion through it, scheduled between more pleasurable pastimes.

Prayer is also an integral part of Bible study, for it prepares our hearts to hear what God is saying. If we take it seriously, listening to God will be exciting.

All Christians need to be taught. We need to learn the proper conduct at home, at school, in the workplace, while shopping, while traveling, in a medical facility. We need to know how to react in the face of adverse circumstances.

God uses the sermons and messages of godly teachers to guide us. When we hear and read the Word of God, we need to set our hearts and minds to stand at full attention. The God of the universe is speaking. The Holy Spirit of God energizes our minds to gain insight into God's Word. That's why it's good to be seated in the pew on Sunday mornings, as well as at other times of worship. As God speaks through his Spirit-filled minister, you will discover answers to your personal questions regarding your walk with God. God knows each of us that well.

A fellow Christian shared that, as a new convert, she received answers to questions she held in her heart every Sunday morning as the Word of God was preached. It seemed as if the minister were speaking to her alone. Another shared that he received the long-sought solution to a problem when he visited a church one Sunday morning. I have learned how to handle many everyday matters while listening to the Word of God. Such testimonials could go on and on.

God speaks to each heart. We must continually listen and obey his Word. When we do, life can be lived in a state of eternal blessedness, because we are never without the voice of God.

God will speak to our deepest needs. I experienced this early in my walk with him, for he knew what I truly needed. One evening when I was living what I considered a tedious life, I begged him to give me strength to go on. I asked him to add something to my life. I left the decision as to what he would add up to him, and I wondered how he would answer.

I didn't have to wait long to find out. When I awoke the next morning, it was as if I saw an open Bible with these words: *So shall the Word of God, yielding power, give power unto you.* It wasn't the type of answer I expected, and I didn't realize it at the time, but by turning my attention to his Word, God was answering my actual deepest need. He knew I needed his power. I could only receive it through faith in his Word.

I read the Bible from cover to cover in one week. This fast-track read did not allow for total absorption, of course, but the picture of God and his Word began to emerge more clearly. I saw him lead Moses and Joshua. I watched him work wonders through Moses. I heard him speak to Abraham, Jacob, and Samuel. I heard him speak through the prophets. I grew to know that I needed the power of God in my life to live and work for him. Our need for God is revealed in his Word. He wants all of us to hear and to heed it.

Sometimes, to get our attention, God will allow us to feel pain at the depths of our emotions. When we are attentive, he will guide us. He'll give us our desire, or he'll give us what is best, according to his will. God knew best how to bless Paul when, instead of granting Paul's request, he said, "My grace is sufficient for thee: for my strength is made perfect in weakness" (2 Corinthians 12:9).

The Holy Spirit will minister by bringing to our minds that portion of Scripture that meets an immediate need. We have the promise Jesus made many years ago: "But the Comforter, which is the Holy Ghost, whom the Father will send in my name, he shall teach you all things, and bring all things to your remembrance, whatsoever I have said unto you" (John 14:26).

Lying awake in the warm silent darkness of an early morning in July, I needlessly worried about how I would find the school, almost twenty miles from my home, where God was leading me to study. My worry was needless because God had already led me to the point of turning in paperwork, strictly by faith, before a short hospital stay. Surely he could take care of getting me to the school.

But that wasn't my thinking at the time, and I didn't see God moving by my schedule. The date of my appointment

✝

with an advisor was only two weeks away, and I didn't even have an idea of which direction to steer the car. I knew that the best solution was to find and ride with someone who knew the directions so I could learn the route. As I lay in bed, God spoke to my anxiety, from 2 Corinthians 9:8, to assure me that he would make all sufficiency abound toward me, and he reinforced his assurance with words from Philippians 4:19, reminding me that the Lord would supply all my needs.

Later the same morning, I rode with my mother to a grocery store that was several miles away. As we drove into the parking lot, just ahead I saw a sign against the blue sunlit sky, signaling that the school was just down the road ahead. I'd had no idea the ride would take me near the school. My mother had been unaware that I needed to know the location of this campus. A faithful God was faithful in acting according to his promises. His Word is true. We can always place complete trust in God. Hold on by faith to his Word. Whether the evidence of his work comes instantly or through circumstances that work out more slowly, as we listen to God and trust in him, we'll see him working for our good.

God wants our ultimate trust. As I rode a bus to work one morning, God brought this to my mind: *God knows my every need.* On a Sunday after church, he spoke to my mind these words: *Jesus is all I need.*

God has always shown himself as the provider of all our needs. He provided food for Adam and Eve in the garden of Eden (Genesis 2:16); he rained bread from heaven for the children of Israel (Exodus 16); he fed Elijah when he led Elijah to hide himself, providing food and water daily (1 Kings 17:2–6); he fed Elijah in the wilderness many days (1 Kings 19:5–8); he prepared a gourd to shelter Jonah (Jonah 4:6).

God will often guide us toward an action or undertaking through a strong conviction or desire. We learn to listen for his answers to our prayers, knowing he will never lead us in a direction that is contrary to his Word. Bible study, prayer, and meditation are indispensable. Knowing what the Scriptures say and learning about the character of God helps us to discern when God is speaking to us.

For example, God will never lead any of us to fulfill that dream of opening our own restaurant with money knowingly received because of error by bank, employer, or any other source. The Word of God clearly says that stealing in any form is wrong. We must pray about the desire to start that business, go on that missionary journey, or whatever the endeavor. If it's God's will, he will strengthen the conviction or desire and go before us opening doors and guiding us from vision to realization.

Before I owned my first car, I dreamed of owning one. But not just any car—it had to be a Ford Pinto. Every time I saw one of them, I dreamed of being the driver. But that was another dream because I didn't drive. Therefore, I wasn't sure it was time to buy a car. But God knew the dream and he knew the time to fulfill it. He knew when to let me hear him speak.

One lunch break, Miriam, a coworker, invited me to come with her to shop for her first car. The car dealer would pick us up. Since I had nothing better to do for the next hour, I accepted the invitation.

As the three of us walked around the lot on the warm, partly sunny November day, it wasn't long before Miriam found her car, a mustard-colored Pinto. (Wouldn't it have to be a Pinto!) In the meantime, a used white Pinto with a red and blue hood caught my eye, and that's where it stayed. As salespersons will, he noticed my interest, and began working toward making another sale. No need to worry about my lack of a driver's license; he would personally deliver the car to my home.

During the next few days, I prayed for God's guidance. Not only did I crave a Pinto, but I also needed a car. But my apprehensions were in control. I needed to hear from God.

Within a couple of days I knew with certainty that God was controlling the circumstances. He had placed in me the desire to own a car, and had led me to a car. Now was the time to buy it. I became the owner of a 1972 Pinto.

But within me, everything was not settled. When I gazed out the window at the car sitting in the driveway, fear took over. I saw a huge red, white, and blue alien-looking machine sitting unwelcome in my space. What would I do with it? While some would have eagerly jumped into the driver's seat, I wasn't ready. The Holy Spirit brought a verse to my mind: "And we know that all things work together for good to them that love God, to them who are the called according to his purpose" (Romans 8:28).

These words made me aware that God was with me, sharing my concern. The thought helped me know everything would work out.

Of course, my fear turned out to be senseless. I soon learned to drive the car and obtained a driver's license. God was teaching me to trust in him, and he had shown me that he knew my need before I brought it before him. "For your Father knoweth what things ye have need of, before ye ask him" (Matthew 6:8).

God was about to bring experiences into my life that would make driving a necessity. He used the situation to help me understand that I needed to let him be the Lord of my life and to trust in him. There was no need to be concerned about my needs being met. As we submit ourselves to God, we'll hear him through his Word. He doesn't want us to fear. He will impart the assurance we need.

God will speak to us through situations we face. As God's children, we take the way of peace, forgiveness, and understanding. When faced with conflict, we draw encouragement and strength from Scriptures such as this: "A soft answer turneth away wrath: but grievous words stir up anger" (Proverbs 15:1).

A few years into my association with a person providing a professional service, God led me to pray for the person. Up to this time, meetings had been mostly pleasant. But after a while, the individual was often rude. I was accused of complaining when I attempted to ask for information. Naturally, my first inclination was to walk away, but there were reasons why I could not yet. God set it that way. I remembered a verse from Proverbs: "The eyes of the Lord are in every place, beholding the evil and the good" (Proverbs 15:3). These words comforted me by reminding me that God was always right in the room with me.

After one difficult session, I reached a breaking point. I left feeling anguish. For the rest of the day and half of the next, I hurt. I could only say to God, "I hurt." I wanted God to take the hurt away. He did. And I received insight that the person I was dealing with needed healing that only God could give. I needed to continue to pray for myself and for the other person, looking to God for strength. All

✝

my apprehension about meeting with the individual had to be handed to God so I could be used by him however he chose.

Sometimes we face uncomfortable situations as we allow God to work through us, but his love and presence will sustain us. God gently led me to love, not accuse, to continue to pray, exercising the forbearance taught in his Word. I thanked God for the turmoil. Through it, he let me experience the peace that prevails in our hearts when we trust and obey him.

We can become lost in laboring for a successful career, a lovely home, or the best car we can afford. We can work hard to be prosperous in whatever project we're working on. But God wants us to hear him say: "Labor not for the meat which perisheth, but for that meat which endureth unto everlasting life" (John 6:27).

God brought this verse to my mind as at home I recalled a discussion at work earlier in the day, when at least two sides disagreed about the menu for an upcoming luncheon. God used this simple scene to help me realize that seeking his kingdom should be life's priority. We find trivial matters important enough to warrant our time and energy, and sometimes they are. But when we leave God out of our lives, our devotion is handed over to temporal matters only. Our labor is in vain.

God must be first in our lives. The Word of God has spoken: "Seek ye first the kingdom of God, and his righteousness; and all these things shall be added unto you" (Matthew 6:33).

If we spend our lives seeking God, he will take care of the other matters. He will lead, he will guide, and he will provide. He will speak. Our responsibility is to listen.

WAIT ON THE LORD

My times are in thy hand.

—Psalm 31:15

T HERE IS NO PURPOSE IN *heaven for which there is no time,* God responded in answer to my impatient asking of *when?* I knew that God had more for me than a nine-to-five workday existence, and in my opinion, it was time for things to start happening. There was church on Sundays and during midweek, but I felt I needed new experiences—the opportunity to travel to new places, meet new people—something besides the same schedule week after week. God's view, of course, was different from mine.

I read this Bible verse: *To every thing there is a season, and a time to every purpose under the heaven* (Ecclesiastes 3:1). This is what God wanted me to hear. I began to listen.

The Bible repeatedly shows God moving in his time to fulfill promises and answer prayers. God promised Abraham that he would bless him and make of him a great nation. Twenty-five years passed before Isaac, the son God promised him, the son through whom the nation would come, was born. Joseph was falsely accused and imprisoned

✝

for years before God brought deliverance. Moses became the avenger when an Egyptian struck one of his Hebrew brothers, but he would have to wait forty years before God established him as the leader he would use to deliver the children of Israel from Egyptian bondage.

God has established a time to move in every situation. There is always a purpose for his timing. It's important that we wait patiently for the answers to our prayers. God not only knows our needs better than we do, but he also knows best both how and the right time to satisfy the need.

At age twenty-nine, events in my life were not moving at the pace I thought they should be, and I spent an entire February day praying to the Lord to make something happen. God brought this to my mind: *Commit thy way unto the Lord ... and he will bring it to pass.* Psalm 37:5 includes these words. I had studied Scripture and had heard many sermons. I was willing to live for God, or so I thought. But I had not given my whole self to him in total commitment. God was teaching me that living for him was not focusing on myself and my desires but on him and his will for me.

Surely God will answer my prayer and quickly involve me in another project, I thought as I prayed on a chilly night in December. I was bored and frustrated. A project that I had been involved in had ended. I needed another right away.

Early the next morning, I received my answer. This time, God used this verse to speak to me: *We count them happy which endure* (James 5:11).

Later the same morning, God brought this thought to my mind: *Trust ye in him at all times.* In the Bible, I read these words: *Trust ye in the Lord for ever: for in the Lord*

Jehovah is everlasting strength (Isaiah 26:4). I was to learn that trusting and waiting yield spiritual strength.

Waiting is a blessing. There is purpose in waiting. I didn't like the answers to my prayers. Each answer actually saddened me, for a while anyway, with the thought that I might as well prepare for no change in my circumstances anytime soon. But what I perceived as disadvantages were turning into blessings. Each time God turned my attention from what I thought I had to have immediately, he was drawing me closer to him.

I grew to know the pain of waiting as a prelude to a shower of great blessings. I learned that God was using the wait to shape me into a vessel he could use. I had to learn, and I am learning, patient endurance. In times of yielded waiting for God, the heart is a fertile ground for learning. Through waiting, God taught me to trust all my life to him. In times when it's hard to wait, hard to trust, trust God anyway. Seek his guidance for using the talent or gift he has given you. Wait for his answer. He'll show you how to use it and open a way for you to do it. Stay in his Word. In the end, you will find joyous praise in your heart for all the blessings he has added to your life as you waited. Wait patiently, confidently. Remember these words from the book of Isaiah:

> He giveth power to the faint; and to them that have no might he increaseth strength. Even the youths shall faint and be weary, and the young men shall utterly fall: But they that wait upon the Lord shall renew their strength; they shall mount up with wings as eagles; they shall run, and not be weary; and they shall walk, and not faint. (Isaiah 40:29–31)

✝

On an October morning, as I prepared for the day, God spoke into my mind: *Wait thou upon God.* These words rest comfortably in my heart: "Turn thou to thy God: keep mercy and judgment, and wait on thy God continually" (Hosea 12:6).

HOLY UNTO GOD

*And ye shall be holy unto me: for I the
Lord am holy, and have severed you from
other people, that ye should be mine*

—Leviticus 20:26

G OD'S STANDARD IS HOLINESS. GOD'S holiness is made
manifest from the beginning to the end of the Holy
Bible. To please God, we must be holy. We must be
consecrated to God, separated from the world. Accepting
Jesus as our Savior is our entrance into holiness.

As we grow spiritually, we grow in holiness. This verse
records a portion of Jesus' prayer to the Father: "Sanctify
them through thy truth: thy word is truth" (John 17:17).

We cannot make ourselves holy. We are made holy by
the cleansing power of the Word of God. We cannot be
holy for a specified period, then revert to old habits, and
then change to a holy way of life again. Just as the Word
of God endures forever, being made holy by God, we are
forever holy.

God placed the words *Be holy* in my mind as I awoke
one morning. At the time, I didn't know a lot about what it
meant to be holy, but I was willing to learn, and God was
ready to teach me. I listened at church and learned that

✝

holy people don't share the world's values. We don't follow
the latest fads. The way we dress is different. Holy people
are separated, severed from the world and its values. Holy
people deny themselves, putting away unclean habits, to
follow Christ.

Paul admonished the Corinthian Church to separate
themselves from unbelievers, for they did not follow the
way of God. God's promise was that he would be their
Father, and they would be his sons and daughters. Paul
provided excellent motivation for electing a life of growing
in holiness: "Having therefore these promises, dearly
beloved, let us cleanse ourselves from all filthiness of the
flesh and spirit, perfecting holiness in the fear of God" (2
Corinthians 7:1).

Paul had a reminder for the Ephesians: "Be renewed in
the spirit of your mind; and … put on the new man, which
after God is created in righteousness and true holiness"
(Ephesians 4:23–24).

Living in God's holiness, we groom ourselves, but
without following the fashion fads of the world. God loves
inner beauty. Fancy or expensive attire does not win God's
favor. A heart cleansed by the blood of his Son does.

Whose adorning let it not be that outward adorning
of plaiting the hair, and of wearing of gold, or of
putting on of apparel;

But let it be the hidden man of the heart, in that
which is not corruptible, even the ornament of a
meek and quiet spirit, which is in the sight of God
of great price. (1 Peter 3:3–4)

God gave me a lesson in holy living after I attempted
to seize a space in a lunchtime department store crowd

gathered around a counter, where a famous model was sharing tips on the correct way to apply makeup. That evening, as I recalled the event, God brought this verse to my mind: "Little children, keep yourselves from idols" (1 John 5:21). God was teaching me that I was not to allow either people or things to become obsessions. Obsessive thoughts begin to fill our minds and our time instead of God.

On another day, at the same store, a shoe salesman counseled me on my choice of shoes, steering me away from shoes that had the appearance of the "dance hall." He was a missionary and thought a more conservative style would be more becoming. Years later, I still thank God for his lesson through the shoe salesman.

In rendering service before God, whether it is singing in the choir, passing the collection plate, cleaning the floors of the sanctuary, or teaching Sunday school, we should reflect on the great privilege of honoring the Holy and Sovereign God. Serve him with reverence and fear. The ancient priests who brought offerings before God on behalf of the people had to undergo ceremonial cleansing before approaching the Holy God: "They shall be holy unto their God, and not profane the name of their God: for the offerings of the Lord made by fire, and the bread of their God, they do offer: therefore they shall be holy" (Leviticus 21:6).

One January day, God blessed me with guidance on devoting my all to him when he brought to me these words: *When you offer offerings in the presence of the Lord your God, you shall be holy.* He was teaching me to appreciate the seriousness and dedication with which I must render service. I did not know that I was about to be called upon to render service.

Later in the same month, my Sunday school teacher offered me the opportunity to be student teacher for one class meeting. The next month, my pastor approached me about becoming an assistant Sunday school teacher. I accepted both assignments, recalling the words the Holy Spirit had spoken and awed by the God who had gone before, preparing me. Any offering we make to God—time, talent, money, anything—although it may seem small, it should bring glory to God.

Holy people are especially blessed. God called the children of Israel, a people with a special relationship to him, his special treasure: "Thou art a holy people unto the Lord thy God: the Lord thy God hath chosen thee to be a special people unto himself, above all people that are upon the face of the earth" (Deuteronomy 7:6).

God instructed Moses to say this to the children of Israel:

"If ye will obey my voice indeed, and keep my covenant, then ye shall be a peculiar treasure unto me above all people: for all the earth is mine: And ye shall be unto me a kingdom of priests, and a holy nation" (Exodus 19:5–6).

God's call today is still that we live holy lives. Peter spoke of the church: "But ye are a chosen generation, a royal priesthood, a holy nation, a peculiar people; that ye should show forth the praises of him who hath called you out of darkness into his marvelous light" (1 Peter 2:9).

It is God's will that we come out of the darkness of sin into the light of spiritual truth. He has commanded us to be holy. The decision as to whether or not to obey and have an abundant life is ours. God's way is true treasure.

FAITH

And Jesus answering saith unto
them, Have faith in God.

—Mark 11:22

FAITH SUSTAINS US THROUGHOUT OUR walk with God. We are saved by faith when we believe that Jesus died for us and we accept his gift of grace. Like Abraham, we are declared righteous through faith. By faith in God, we grow in righteousness and holiness. Our faith is tested as God molds us into the persons he wants us to be.

Faith sustains us through all of life's struggles. I like the way that Hannah, after being informed by Eli the priest that her prayer had been answered, left sadness behind as she left the place of worship, although she had not yet seen the evidence of her answered prayer (1 Samuel. 1:18). I often think about the faith that the widow of Zarephath had to exercise as she obeyed Elijah, the man of God, feeding him first when she had barely enough to prepare what she considered one last meal for herself and her son. Her faith and obedience were greatly rewarded (1 Kings 17:8–16).

My heart is lifted when I see King Jehoshaphat look beyond the enemy forces invading Judah and to the Lord.

✝

He also directed all of Judah to trust in God: "Believe in the Lord your God, so shall ye be established; believe his prophets, so shall ye prosper" (2 Chronicles 20:20).

He directed them to praise the Lord for the victory even before the enemy was defeated: "And when they began to sing and to praise, the Lord set ambushments against the children of Ammon, Moab, and mount Seir, which were come against Judah; and they were smitten" (2 Chronicles 20:22).

Similarly, the people followed Joshua's lead, and on the seventh day of marching around the wall of the city of Jericho, they shouted the victory shout because faith said that the city of Jericho, the most well-known city in the region, was defeated. At their shout, the wall surrounding the city fell flat (Joshua 6).

The children of Israel sought guidance from the Lord before going to battle with the tribe of Benjamin (Judges 20). Should they fight the battle? God said yes. They fought. They were defeated. They asked God again if they should fight, this time with weeping. Again God said yes. Again they were defeated. They went before God again. This time they wept, and fasted, and offered burnt offerings and peace offerings. Phinehas the priest went before God to ask if the children of Israel should go to battle once more. The answer was yes—and this time God promised to deliver the enemy into their hands. God, of course, was faithful to his Word, and the enemy was defeated.

The Israelites persisted in faith until they saw victory. So must we. We want to come with humbled hearts, knowing we can do nothing without God. We come with humbled hearts cleansed by Jesus' blood.

Simon had been fishing all night, but his nets were still empty when Jesus sat down in his ship. When Jesus encouraged Simon to let down his nets into the deep water for a catch, Simon informed Jesus of the hours he'd already worked and how he had nothing to show for his time. "Nevertheless at thy word I will let down the net" (Luke 5:5).

I like the way Simon transitioned from focusing on not seeing any chance of the fish biting to obedience. Faith and obedience are inseparable. In both Old and New Testament times, when someone had faith to obey a direction from God, results followed.

In the pages of the Bible, we witness people having faith in their hearts and believing in God's power through Jesus. Without a direct call to action from God, they exercised their faith. The book of Matthew tells of the centurion who asked Jesus to heal his servant. The centurion reasoned that if he had authority over the men under him, certainly Jesus, whose authority extended over all things, could intervene and heal his servant: "Speak the word only, and my servant shall be healed" (Matthew 8:8). Jesus commended his great faith and rewarded it with the healing of the servant. The woman with an issue of blood had sought healing for years. The day came when she had a chance to get close to Jesus. She knew her healing was within reach: "She said within herself, If I may but touch his garment, I shall be whole" (Matthew 9:21). She was healed.

Early in my faith journey, God gave me a special lesson about how faith leads to victory. I had looked for my first job for more than a year. It seemed the job would never materialize. I listened to the sermon about faith during a Sunday morning service. A special time of prayer

✝

was to follow that evening. The pastor encouraged the congregation to have faith that God could meet any need. Like the woman who knew that she would be healed if she touched the hem of Jesus' garment, I believed that if I got into the prayer that evening, I would find a job.

All Sunday afternoon, I couldn't wait to get back to church for the prayer. I arrived at the scheduled time, and when the prayer began, I prayed with faith that God would answer. The next week, the newspaper ad that was to bring my opportunity appeared. I responded and was hired. God had blessed me to hear his Word with faith in my heart. My need was met.

God allowed me to witness firsthand what it means to believe in him as the supplier of all needs. Just believe. He is faithful. God desires that we look at what cannot be seen. That's faith. We see it not with physical eyes but by faith. Next, the evidence appears.

Walking in righteousness by faith in God, we share a blessing with Abraham, of whom the Scripture says: "And he believed in the Lord; and he counted it to him for righteousness" (Genesis 15:6).

Paul described God's blessing on believers of today: "So then they which be of faith are blessed with faithful Abraham" (Galatians 3:9).

Righteous people are especially blessed of God, as witnessed in the Scriptures.

"The Lord loveth the righteous" (Psalm 146:8). He delights in those who serve him.

"The righteous shall flourish like the palm tree: he shall grow like a cedar in Lebanon" (Psalm 92:12).

Righteous people obey the Word of God. Therefore is this blessing bestowed: "Blessed are they that hear the word of God, and keep it" (Luke 11:28).

God gives us a vitality that we can receive from no other source. Joy abides in the heart of the righteous. Unlike happiness, which is based on circumstances, joy can abide when the bills are not paid. God's people witness that joy can be present when it seems everything is going wrong. One of the first experiences with joy that I remember was at a time when I needed an automobile part that wasn't immediately available. I certainly wasn't happy in the situation. In fact, I was saddened. Yet bubbling within me was a joyous feeling that I could not explain. I recall thinking, *Why do I feel "happy" when I feel so bad?* I did not control the feeling; God did. With God's help, my problem was resolved sooner than I expected. I had to thank God for that, as well as for the joy. The more we stay in God's Word, the more joy there is.

We can manufacture neither righteousness nor joy. Both are dependent on faith in God. It's good to do good, but good deeds are no substitute for righteousness. For someone who has not experienced it, the blessed life of the righteous may be hard to comprehend, for appearance is many times the opposite of reality. With minimal material possessions, and with simplicity rather than lavishness, people who live righteously by faith in God are so blessed of God that they testify of feeling as if they are sitting in the palace of a king. The contentment that comes from God cannot be bought.

"For whatsoever is born of God overcometh the world: and this is the victory that overcometh the world, even our faith" (1 John 5:4). Faith in God empowers us to live for him.

✝

The Bible says that we become new when we believe his Word and accept Jesus. We don't succumb to sin because of his power, which gives a victorious life in Christ.

WISDOM

Wisdom is the principal thing;
therefore get wisdom:
and with all thy getting get understanding.

—Proverbs 4:7

G OD SPOKE INTO MY MIND early one morning, saying, *Wisdom comes only from God.* So teaches the Holy Bible. God had previously cautioned me: *You cannot take wisdom away from God and assign it to any other source.* When he brought me a passage from the Bible on the subject of wisdom, it was one that clearly identifies him as its source: "For the Lord giveth wisdom: out of his mouth cometh knowledge and understanding. He layeth up sound wisdom for the righteous: he is a buckler to them that walk uprightly" (Proverbs 2:6–7).

God urges us to listen, to know where to look for life's wisdom. Other verses in the book of Proverbs explain why it is important to possess wisdom and press us to seek it as "silver and hid treasures." Silver, as a precious metal as well as "treasure," conjures up visions of things we strive to hold on to because of their value. Wisdom is set in a lofty place. To seek wisdom, we must seek God. To increase in wisdom, we must remain steadfast in God's Word.

✝

As children of God, we have Jesus living within us through the Holy Spirit. Jesus embodies the wisdom of God: "Of him are ye in Christ Jesus, who of God is made unto us wisdom, and righteousness, and sanctification, and redemption" (1 Cor. 1:30).

When we reject the Word of God and God's gift of salvation through Jesus Christ, we reject the only way to true wisdom. Jeremiah said these words of the wise men of Judah: "The wise men are ashamed, they are dismayed and taken: lo, they have rejected the word of the Lord; and what wisdom is in them?" (Jeremiah 8:9).

God brought another Scripture to me: "The Lord knoweth the thoughts of the wise, that they are vain" (1 Corinthians 3:20). Man's wisdom, he cautions, is vain. The Scriptures also testify this: "The wisdom of this world is foolishness with God" (1 Corinthians 3:19).

What wisdom is there after the wisdom of God is rejected? When we need help, we need God. Our own wisdom is limited by our finite understanding. God chose to make us dependent on him to guide us through the affairs of life. It's comforting to know that we don't have to roam aimlessly. The wisdom of God is our guide.

Parents may acquire valuable knowledge from books and magazine articles to help in child rearing. But if the wisdom God gives is left out, the child may not be raised in the fear of the Lord. Parents will miss the advantage of the wisdom God is ready to impart to aid in understanding and guiding each child in the family. God has the supreme knowledge. He knows his plan for each person.

God's wisdom will lead us away from habits such as gambling, which are the consequence of a lack of trust in God. God's wisdom teaches us how to live peacefully, when to speak and when to be silent, how to dress, how to be fair and just. God's wisdom helps the employer deal with employees and teaches employees how to deal with the employer and with one another. Wisdom keeps us from entangling ourselves in unhealthy or unseemly relationships.

The wisdom of God helps us identify crutches in our lives. His power will help us put them away. God's wisdom helps us discern between good and evil.

"There is no wisdom nor understanding nor counsel against the Lord" (Proverbs 21:30). Bible study opens a vast store of wisdom. But we can't reach this wisdom without God's help. God alone can give us insight into his Word. Reading the Word of God without God in our lives is a completely different experience from reading it after we have received Christ. The intellect of the unbelieving heart may know the meaning of words in general, but as physical blindness obscures sight, spiritual blindness makes understanding the truth of the Word of God impossible.

"When he, the Spirit of truth, is come, he will guide you into all truth" (John 16:13). The Holy Spirit sheds light on God's Word and teaches us to apply it to our lives. As we seek wisdom, we have help in deciding whether we should join a social group. God's wisdom helps us determine whether a form of entertainment is appropriate. When we seek godly wisdom, we please God.

Many of us first heard about the Wisdom of Solomon in our early Sunday school days. We witnessed him judging the dispute between the two women who both claimed the living infant. The son of one had died. Which was the mother of the living infant? Solomon judged in the wisdom God gave him.

✝

God gave wisdom to all those he called as they carried out the ministry he called them to. The apostle Paul, a powerful minister, depended on God's wisdom. All his discourses were based on wisdom he received from God (see 2 Peter 3:15).

We grow in wisdom as we become more familiar with the Word of God. Listen to God. Listen to the voice of God's servants from the pulpit. Study the Bible and pray. You will learn to walk in wisdom. Life will be much richer.

HONOR THE LORD WITH PRAISE

Thine, O Lord, is the greatness, and the power, and the glory, and the victory, and the majesty: for all that is in the heaven and in the earth is thine; thine is the kingdom, O Lord, and thou art exalted as head above all. Both riches and honor come of thee, and thou reignest over all; and in thine hand is power and might; and in thine hand it is to make great, and to give strength unto all. Now therefore, our God, we thank thee, and praise thy glorious name.

—1 Chronicles 29:11–13

THIS FIRST PORTION OF DAVID'S prayer is majestic praise to God. We owe God praise. "Praise ye the Lord: for it is good to sing praises unto our God; for it is pleasant; and praise is comely" (Psalm 147:1).

Praise is comely. God placed these words in my mind during praise service one evening at church. Later at home, I read the words from Psalm 147. I also read this verse: "Rejoice in the Lord, O ye righteous: for praise is comely for the upright" (Psalm 33:1).

✝

No activity is nobler than praising God. We don't have to recall the last great thing we feel God did for us in order to begin praising him. We praise him because he is God. I was thinking of praise as always proper—when I feel good, when I don't feel good, when evil seems to be triumphing—and God brought clearly to my mind, in praise to him, *Thou art my praise.*

God delights in the praise of the righteous because he loves righteous people. It is God's will that we rejoice not in the gates of wickedness but in the gates of righteousness and holiness. God does not want lip service. God brought to my mind a passage from the book of Matthew, and it urges us to remember that insincere praise in any form displeases God: "This people draw nigh unto me with their mouth, and honor me with their lips; but their heart is far from me" (Matthew 15:8). Jesus spoke these words in rebuke of religious leaders who rejected him.

Times of gathering for worship are special times for God's people to honor him with thanksgiving and praise. We dress in our Sunday best to honor and worship God. With all the cares and worries of the world shut out, God's people lift their voices in song and praise. Hearts are touched by God. "The joy of the Lord is your strength" (Nehemiah 8:10).

There's joy in praise. Listening to the Word of God produces joy in the hearts of believers. Joy produces praise, and praise produces joy. Both joy and praise bring strength. As we let go of problems and sorrows during praise, we are renewed. God strengthens us to continue life's journey.

When our praise is sincere, our lives continue to praise God outside of the church building. We live to his glory. In the attitude of praise, we don't become angry or frustrated when someone snatches our parking space, or when a store clerk not feeling so well on Monday is rude or when we don't get the promotion we're aching for. With hearts of praise, we thank God anyway, for he is always the same Almighty God. He gives us the power to pray for strength for ourselves, that we will continue to stand and pray for, as well as forgive, those whose actions may have caused us inconvenience or pain.

God deserves praise. We owe God praise. "I will bless the Lord at all times: his praise shall continually be in my mouth" (Psalm 34:1).

Given to me of God, I will bow down to him and the majesty of his power. His power is great—above all.

FROM DAY TO DAY

I

"What is good—Jesus?" The boy paused from rolling a toy truck across the apartment's living room carpet. His position between the television, tuned to a Sunday afternoon sermon, and his grandmother and great aunt as they discussed the minister's message in the small dining area behind him, was not a good place to command attention.

The two women, their attention divided between the television and their own conversation, did not hear the boy's question. Respectfully not interrupting the adult conversation, he returned to playing silently. Although it wasn't intentional, the opportunity to teach a child about God was missed that afternoon. The Bible teaches us the Word of God is an integral part of the daily lives of children as well as adults: "And ye shall teach them your children, speaking of them when thou sittest in thine house, and when thou walkest by the way, when thou liest down, and when thou risest up" (Deuteronomy 11:19).

Parents and other adult family members are responsible for teaching children about God. We make a valuable investment when we immerse ourselves in the Word of God. When we lead a child to faith, we help build a new godly generation.

II

As I stopped at the traffic light, I noticed the maroon SUV in the driveway of the store parking lot to my right. The huge vehicle, or so it seemed in proportion to my compact car, was inching outward, toward the space between my vehicle and the car directly ahead of me. Roll, stop, roll, stop. I watched the movement of the vehicle, aiming for the space my car was within inches of occupying.

The light changed from red to green. The car ahead began to roll forward. The SUV seized the spot on the black pavement I should have owned. I was left waiting as the light changed to red again, watching the huge vehicle make it across the intersection. I felt a twinge of hurt. My wheels, not those of the SUV, should have been rolling.

Sitting at the traffic light, I began to think, "Isn't this what living for God is all about? Love thy neighbor as thyself" (Matthew 19:19); "Charity suffereth long, and is kind" (1 Corinthians 13:4).

Sure, the other driver could have waited until the minimally busy street cleared to drive out of the parking lot, saving me the minor inconvenience of missing the light. But the incident turned into a blessing. I sat captured in the light of truth. Thanks to God, there is a standard. There are inalterable rules for living, set by God. We don't have to wonder, we have the ability to know what is right. All we need is the desire to listen to God; He will teach.

For God so loved the world, that he gave his only begotten Son, that whosoever believeth in him should not perish, but have everlasting life. (John 3:16)

He that loveth not knoweth not God; for God is love. (1 John 4:8)

Love gives. If love gives, love gives in. When love gives in, God's love is demonstrated.

III

Two small boys stood in an aisle at the dollar store, looking at a toy that would soon belong to them. As the younger boy held the shrink-wrapped package, the older child, about seven, assured him, "We'll play with it when we get home." With dreamy anticipation in his voice, he repeated, "When we get home."

Later, recalling the scene reminded me of the Christian's hope. *When we get home.*

Eternal life and joy await us in our heavenly home, where God himself will dwell with us forever. Revelation 21:4 assures us that there will be no more death, no more sorrow, no more crying, no more pain. We learn in Revelation 21:5 that this promise is made by a true and faithful God, and so it cannot be altered.

When we receive Jesus as our Savior, we receive the promise of eternal blessings in our eternal home. Christians can indeed anticipate a time of great joy— *when we get home.*

IV

I waited for the traffic light to change to green. A long wait, it seemed, in the warm September sunshine, which made its presence known even with cool air streaming from the air vents. Out of the corner of my left eye, I noticed a motorized chair crossing the street and heading in my direction. I glanced at the light. Still red. Turning around to see the chair, I noticed the woman seated in it. I noticed the breathing tube in her nose. She approached my car and motioned for me to open the window.

"Can you help me? I have only one can of spinach in my cabinet. My social security check doesn't come until next week."

I glanced at the light, thinking I would not have time to reach into my purse and place something in her hand. The light was about to change. The light changed—to green. I started to place my foot on the gas pedal and take off. I looked at the woman again and forgot the traffic light. I reached for my purse.

I said to her, "God bless you. I'll pray for you." She smiled and rolled back across the street.

I looked at the traffic light. It changed again—to red. I glanced into my rearview mirror. No one was behind me. Thank you, Lord. I had not delayed anyone.

The light changed to green again. I drove away feeling much more content than I would have if I had sped away with the first green light, leaving my duty behind.

There is no room for thinking of self first in the kingdom of God. If Jesus had thought only of himself, he would not have endured the suffering of the cross. What was my little delay in comparison to that? God once gave me this thought: *You give yourself to God that you may give yourself for others.* Lord, I'm learning to walk in your way.

"I was an hungered, and ye gave me meat" (Matthew 25:35).

V

Sometimes when a behavior is being considered, the question "Is that a sin?" is asked. The question may be a sign of a lack of understanding. We have to remember that we come into the world as sinners by nature and remain that way until we accept God's gift of salvation through Jesus Christ. Before taking this step, we may depend on good deeds and good moral choices to be good persons. But good moral choices and good deeds do not constitute salvation. Therefore, making the right choice does not change a person's status from sinner to saint.

When we are saved, God takes away the taste for sinful pleasures. Our inner guide, the Holy Spirit, helps us distinguish between good and evil. As we sit under godly teaching, we grow in this grace. If we discover, through the Word of God, that we don't measure up to God's standards, we seek God for the power to change. We are never left to live on the shaky ground of "I don't know if I'm sinning or not …" The concern should not be "Is this a sin?" but "Am I a sinner in the eyes of God?"

Good moral choices are commendable, but they can't make us pleasing to God. Morals don't give us power over sin. Morals don't give us eternal life. Jesus came to reconcile sinful people to God. Jesus is the only way to God. It would be tragic not to inherit the eternal life God has given us through Jesus Christ, for morals rather than God become our guide to righteousness.

God sent not his Son into the world to condemn the world; but that the world through him might be saved. He that believeth on him is not condemned: but he that believeth not is condemned already, because he hath not believed in the name of the only begotten Son of God. (John 3:17–18)

VI

A man gathering sticks portrays a peaceful scene (Numbers 15). No hint of anything disturbing enters the picture. There's only quietness, complete serenity. Yet something is wrong. Something unseen is lurking in the picture. That something is sin.

The man gathering sticks is violating God's law. There was nothing wrong with the act of gathering sticks. But the act was being performed on the Sabbath Day. God had commanded that no work be done on the Sabbath.

> Six days shalt thou labor, and do all thy work: But the seventh day is the sabbath of the Lord thy God: in it thou shalt not do any work, thou, nor thy son, nor thy daughter, thy manservant, nor thy maidservant, nor thy cattle, nor thy stranger that is within thy gates:
>
> For in six days the Lord made heaven and earth, the sea, and all that in them is, and rested the seventh day: wherefore the Lord blessed the sabbath day, and hallowed it. (Exodus 20:9–11)

Disobeying the law carried a consequence. Disobedience required punishment: "Ye shall keep the sabbath therefore; for it is holy unto you: every one that defileth it shall surely be put to death: for whosoever doeth any work therein, that soul shall be cut off from among his people" (Exodus 31:14).

The man did not escape the punishment. He was stoned to death.

Life sometimes portrays the serenity of the picture of the man picking up sticks. Our lives are comfortable, almost perfect. We have all we need and all we want. We feel sheltered from whatever might harm us. We have it all. But something unseen exists in the picture. The unseen something is sin that is not readily apparent. If God does not rule our lives, sin is in the picture. We, like the man gathering sticks, will have to suffer the consequences of disobeying God's Word.

God has entrusted final judgment to his Son Jesus Christ. Jesus will act within that authority.

> In flaming fire taking vengeance on them that know not God, and that obey not the gospel of our Lord Jesus Christ: Who shall be punished with everlasting destruction from the presence of the Lord, and from the glory of his power; When he shall come to be glorified in his saints, and to be admired in all them that believe. (2 Thessalonians 1:8—10)

Every life needs Jesus to cleanse sin from the picture. The picture will then be like treasure in the eyes of God.

VII

It is good for me that I have been afflicted;
that I might learn thy statutes.

—*Psalm 119:71*

God knows the value of affliction. He will allow us to hurt, to yearn, to feel empty, to feel lonely—all to help us grow closer to him. During times of affliction, we learn to trust God; we grow to know his love for us. We are strengthened as our endurance is tested, while God lovingly takes us through to the end of the time of testing. "My brethren, count it all joy when ye fall into divers temptations; knowing this, that the trying of your faith worketh patience" (James 1:2–3).

We grow to know that before the trial is ended that when it's over, we'll see the glorious results of God working in us. Thus we can have joy of heart even during the trials of affliction. God does everything in his love to strengthen and to approve those who serve him.

CLAIMING THE TREASURE

The kingdom of heaven is like unto
treasure hid in a field; the which when
a man hath found, he hideth, and for
joy thereof goeth and selleth all that
he hath, and buyeth that field.

—*Matthew 13:44*

IN GOD, WE HAVE PURE treasure. The man described in the verse from the book of Matthew was willing to give up all he had in exchange for that treasure. When we see Jesus giving up the glory he had with God the Father and taking on human form to suffer a cruel death to redeem a sinful world, we are reminded of the pricelessness of the kingdom of God.

We also need to be willing to give up everything that stands in the way of a relationship with God, even the very things or persons that mean the world to us. God is telling us to come and be saved. God is telling us to be holy. His Word tells us how. The treasure he has for us can be ours. But he left it up to us. Ours is to listen to him. Ours is to obey his Word. We have to value it above all. It is our treasure from God. Who would not want to claim treasure?

✝

Help is always available as we claim our heavenly riches. We can read what God is telling us in the Holy Bible. We can listen as the Word is taught and preached. We can request God's help through prayer. We can meet personally with pastors, ministers, and teachers of the Word of God.

As we walk the path of obedience, God will gently guide. We learn to hear his voice as we learn to obey.

But before we can hear God's voice, we must hear his call to surrender our lives to him. We must receive the gift of salvation that God has provided through the death of Jesus Christ so that our sins may be forgiven. Then he will live in us through his Holy Spirit. Then he will hear our petitions and work for us. He has the power to resolve any problem any of us will ever face, and he always answers on time to meet our needs. We learn to trust him as we learn to hear his voice.

We become possessors of inner peace and joy, as well as eternal life—true treasure, when we listen to the voice of God.